THE INSPIRED CHOICE

Chronicles of Transformation: Horizons Ahead

Volume 2

Caroline Biesalski

The Inspired Choice

Chronicles of Transformation: Horizons Ahead

Caroline Biesalski

Foreword by Norman Gräter

Bibliografische Information der Deutschen Nationalbibliothek:
Die Deutsche Nationalbibliothek verzeichnet diese Publikation
in der Deutschen Nationalbibliografie; detaillierte
bibliografische Daten sind im Internet über http://dnb.dnb.de
abrufbar.

Publisher: BoD · Books on Demand GmbH, In de Tarpen 42,
22848 Norderstedt, bod@bod.de

Print: Libri Plureos GmbH, Friedensallee 273, 22763 Hamburg

ISBN: 978-3-7693-3836-2

CONTENTS

I

"How do I attract interesting guests to my podcast?" is the ultimate question. Sending a generic message like, "Hi, I found your homepage and think you're interesting…" won't get you far. The golden rule for inviting and engaging guests is simple: everyone wants to feel seen, heard, and respected.

This means you need to genuinely invest time in your potential guest. What are their interests, hobbies, or family life? Social media often holds the key. Use this insight to build a connection. Shared interests, values, or visions create bonds, and even small commonalities can overcome vast social or geographical distances.

Picture yourself in the Australian Outback. You're in a dusty bar and overhear someone speaking your language. Back home, you might ignore it, but here, that commonality is invaluable, sparking a conversation. Similarly, uncovering shared ground with your podcast guests can build trust and engagement.

Preparation – A Tip from Larry King
Once your guest confirms, preparation is the next step. Talk-show legend Larry King once said: "I only think of the opening question. After that, I'm curious and just listen." This approach may sound simple, but it's transformative. Early in my podcast journey, I failed at this. I would prepare a list of 1.5 pages of questions and focus on the next query instead of my guest's response. The result? The conversation felt robotic. Today, I know the key to meaningful dialogue is genuine listening and spontaneous curiosity.

What if the Guest is Reserved?
Think of captivating shows like *Lost*. Initially, it might seem underwhelming, but as you discover the characters' backstories, struggles, and goals, you become hooked. Use this in your podcast: ask guests about their roots, challenges,

or defining experiences. These universal stories foster connection.

Success Tip – Oprah's Lesson
Oprah Winfrey observed that after interviews, even the most powerful figures would ask, "Was I okay?" This reveals a universal need for validation. Keep this in mind: when your guests feel seen, heard, and respected, your podcast will succeed.

Finally, have fun! Your energy sets the tone. *Joy in = joy out.*

Norman Gräter – The Inspirator

HORIZONS AHEAD

In the beginning was the journey, and the journey began with a choice. This choice was the spark of all transformation, the compass that charts the course of our destiny. Through choice, we create meaning; through meaning, we illuminate the path ahead. Every horizon we set our sights on begins with one inspired decision.

Imagination is the helm of this great voyage. As Napoleon Hill wisely observed, "Imagination is the starting point of all creation." It is your boundless ability to envision, to dream, and to steer your life in alignment with those dreams. Like a captain guiding a ship through open waters, your imagination equips you with the tools to navigate challenges, embrace opportunities, and discover unseen shores.

Are you mindful of your thoughts, words, and actions? Like the sails of a ship, they determine the direction of your voyage. Each moment offers you the chance to recalibrate your course, to align with the true north of your purpose, and to claim your role as the captain of your destiny.

The waters may sometimes be rough, the skies unclear, but within you lies the power to steer your ship forward. Trust in your imagination, anchor your heart in gratitude, and let your inspired choices light the way.

What conscious choice will you make today to inspire yourself and those around you? How will you contribute to a better world and expand the horizons of your life's voyage? Each day, each decision, is an opportunity to create ripples of transformation that reach far beyond the horizon.

Welcome aboard this journey of growth, connection, and limitless potential. Together, let's chart a course for a brighter future—one inspired choice at a time.

1. YOUR PODCAST VISION

Before you record a single episode or fine-tune your next show, one crucial element stands between you and podcasting success: a crystal-clear vision. Whether you're starting fresh or refining an existing podcast, your vision is your compass. It guides your content, engages your audience, and keeps you aligned with your goals. Let's explore how to craft a vision that inspires and directs your journey.

Your vision is the *why* behind your podcast. It's what motivates you to create and what draws listeners in. Without it, you risk losing focus, spreading your energy too thin, or creating content that feels inconsistent. A strong vision allows you to Clarify your purpose, Connect with your audience and Achieve your goals.

If you're new to podcasting, start by asking foundational questions. These help you identify your purpose and shape your content:

1. What is your podcast about?
2. Who is your target audience?
3. Why should people listen to you?
4. What are your podcast goals?

A vision statement is a concise description of your podcast's purpose and goals. It acts as your North Star and can be as simple as:

- *"Our podcast empowers first-time entrepreneurs by sharing actionable business strategies and inspiring success stories."*
- *"We entertain and inform pet owners with humorous stories, expert advice, and interviews with top veterinarians."*

Imagine where you see your podcast in one year, three years, and beyond. Visualize everything—from the number of listeners to the kinds of guests you'll host. Dream big, and at the same time keep your goals attainable. Write down your aspirations and break them into actionable steps.

While clarity is essential, so is adaptability. Podcasting trends evolve, audiences' preferences shift, and your personal growth may lead to new directions. Be willing to revisit and tweak your vision as needed.

A strong podcast vision is the foundation of your success. It keeps you focused, guides your content, and connects you with your audience on a deeper level. Whether you're a beginner or a seasoned podcaster, investing time in defining or refining your vision will pay dividends in the quality and reach of your show. **Start now**, and let your vision guide you to becoming an exceptional host with extraordinary episodes.

In the world of podcasting, one of the most exciting yet challenging aspects is finding the right guests for your show. As a podcast host, your guests are the heart of the value you bring to your audience. In this chapter, we dive into strategies, platforms, and techniques to help you uncover the perfect guests for your show—turning your guest list into a goldmine of inspiration and knowledge.

Before you even begin your search for guests, create an environment that fosters great conversations. Ensure you have time and space, choose a quiet, distraction-free area where you can focus, and approach each interview with a calm and open mindset. Understand your topic and be ready to engage your guest with meaningful questions. As I often say on The Inspired Choice podcast, "Relax, lean back, and prepare to have the best conversation of your life about a topic you love." Start by clarifying your podcast's niche and topics. Think about the subjects that excite you—the ones you can talk about for hours. Once you're clear on your niche, it becomes much easier to identify guests who fit your vision and bring value to your listeners.

Your warmest network often resides in the palm of your hand. Platforms like Facebook, Instagram, TikTok, and YouTube are goldmines for potential guests. Reach out to your connections, beginning with friends, colleagues, or acquaintances who align with your niche. These are your "warm leads." Invite multiple guests for a roundtable conversation. This approach fosters dynamic discussions and diverse perspectives.

For a more targeted approach, explore podcasting platforms and guest directories, such as Matchmaker.fm, which connects podcast hosts with potential guests based on their interests and expertise, or PodMatch, offering a tailored matchmaking service for podcast hosts and guests. Podcast-specific networks often have guest exchange groups or communities dedicated to podcast collaborations. These platforms simplify the process by recommending guests who are actively seeking interview opportunities.

Don't underestimate the power of word-of-mouth. Ask previous guests to recommend one or two contacts who might be interested in appearing on your show. These referrals often lead to high-quality, pre-vetted guests who align with your audience's interests.

Join groups such as "Be a Guest, Find a Guest," which has over 65,000 members. These communities are a treasure trove for finding guests eager to share their expertise. Simply browse posts or create your own invitation for guest collaborations.

Make scheduling and communication effortless by using a calendar tool. Share a booking link so guests can choose a convenient time for recording, and designate specific days and times for interviews to maintain consistency and balance.

Establish long-term relationships with your guests by following their social media accounts, subscribing to their channels to stay updated and engaged, expressing genuine curiosity about their projects and passions, and exploring collaborations. Every guest is a potential collaborator, client, or advocate for your show.

Not every guest will align with your vision. Build the courage to say no when necessary, ensuring that your podcast remains true to its purpose. As I've learned, having a clear vision makes it easier to make these decisions with confidence.

Remember, finding great guests is about aligning their expertise and energy with your podcast's mission. With the right strategies and tools, your guest list can become a goldmine of insights and inspiration. Stay tuned for the next chapter, where we'll explore how to be a valuable guest and create unforgettable interviews that leave a lasting impact.

3. STANDING OUT IN A CROWDED BOX

In the vast landscape of podcasting, where voices and stories blend into a constant hum, the art of being truly outstanding—whether as a host or a guest—requires intentionality and preparation. Imagine setting aside time in a quiet space, free from distractions, where you can lean back and relax. In that peaceful moment, the conversation transforms into an immersive journey about topics you love, enriched by a guest who brings genuine value and insight. This is the foundation of every memorable interview.

Finding outstanding guests begins with a clear understanding of your niche. When you choose topics that ignite your passion—subjects you can discuss endlessly—you naturally attract individuals whose experiences and expertise resonate with that energy. Start with your warmest contacts: friends, colleagues, and acquaintances from your social media networks. Engage with those you already know, and then expand by exploring guest exchange platforms like matchmaker.fm, PodMatch, or vibrant Facebook groups dedicated to connecting hosts with potential guests. Often, the simplest approach is to ask previous guests for recommendations; one referral can fill your calendar with the right voices.

Beyond the search, establishing a seamless process is crucial. Set up an online calendar link that allows potential guests to book a time effortlessly. Schedule your recording sessions during periods when you know the environment is calm—when pets, kids, or other interruptions are unlikely to disrupt the flow. This preparation isn't just about technical readiness; it's about creating a space where authentic conversation can flourish. When you're fully present, you learn something new with every exchange, and in turn, you pass on that wisdom to your audience.

Yet, standing out isn't solely about the host's efforts. It also means being an outstanding guest on someone else's platform. Whether you are inviting experts or stepping into the interview yourself, it's essential to show genuine interest in your counterpart's work. Follow their social media channels, subscribe to their content, and engage with their community. Such practices foster deeper connections and open the door to future collaborations. Each guest or host is not just a participant in one episode but a potential partner in your ongoing journey of growth and transformation.

Sometimes, the process includes a pre-interview—a chance to gauge the alignment of visions. While pre-interviews can help decide if the chemistry is right, they can also reveal when a conversation isn't the perfect fit. Building the courage to say "no" when necessary is as vital as saying "yes" to opportunities that truly resonate with your mission. In these moments, you are crafting the higher version of yourself, ensuring that every conversation contributes meaningfully to your personal and professional evolution.

Ultimately, being outstanding means embracing the idea that every interview is a chance to learn, to teach, and to connect. It's about setting the intention for what your podcast should be and inviting guests who share that vision. Whether you are hosting or participating, your authenticity and readiness to explore new insights help create an environment where transformative dialogue can take place.

As you continue your podcasting journey, remember that standing out in a crowded box isn't about loud declarations or flashy setups—it's about consistent, thoughtful engagement and the willingness to invest in meaningful conversations. Every step you take in refining your process brings you closer to the heart of authentic storytelling and lasting impact.

4. DEFINING MOMENTS AND EXTRAORDINARY GUESTS

Every journey has defining moments, and my podcasting path has been no exception. In this second volume of *The Inspired Choice Chronicles*, I've had the privilege of hosting an incredible range of guests—successful entrepreneurs, transformative coaches, and truly inspiring individuals—who have not only enriched my life but also helped shape the very mission of *The Inspired Choice.*

Some episodes stand out as milestones, capturing the essence of meaningful dialogue and leaving a lasting impact. I am especially honored to have a foreword written by the Inspirator himself, Norman Gräter. These interviews are more than just recordings—they are reflections of perseverance, authenticity, and the beauty of collaborative learning.

Volume 2 stands out precisely because of these extraordinary guests and the strong sense of purpose they bring. The Inspired Choice podcast has always been about sparking transformation—connecting stories, sharing insights, and embracing the potential each conversation holds. In this chapter, I invite you behind the scenes to discover the lessons, breakthroughs, and inspiration these pivotal moments have provided. May their journeys ignite new possibilities in your own life, just as they have in mine.

To listen to inspiring conversations, check out The Inspired Choice podcast on Spotify, Apple Podcasts, Deezer, Audible, Amazon Music, and other streaming platforms. You can also watch interviews on YouTube.

For the easiest access, visit the podcast website at https://www.podcast.inspiredchoice.today/ and search for the guest's name.

4.1 Audrey Wiggins' – The Power of Connection

As I sat down with Audrey Wiggins for an episode of *Inspired Choice Today*, I quickly realized that I was in the presence of a visionary who has been shaping the worlds of branding, entrepreneurship, and digital media for decades. From her early entrepreneurial ventures at age 15 to her dynamic work as Chief Brand Strategist of Altogether Marketing LLC, Audrey's story is one of resilience, reinvention, and purpose-driven success.

When asked about the one lesson that has stayed with her throughout her career, Audrey's response was simple yet profound: "Believe in the product or service that you sell." This principle, she explained, is the foundation of any successful venture. Without belief, it's impossible to convey the value of what you offer. Her candid reflection on battling imposter syndrome was a reminder that even trailblazers face self-doubt—and that overcoming it is part of the journey.

Audrey's creation of MWMG TV, an on-demand platform for independent content creators, stands as a testament to her innovative spirit. Launched long before video streaming became mainstream, Audrey envisioned a space where creators could showcase their work while accessing the analytics and tools needed to grow their audience. "It's almost like traditional television or Netflix," she explained, highlighting the platform's flexibility and reach. Her early adoption of digital media showcases her ability to see and act on emerging trends.

As a branding expert, Audrey stressed the importance of authenticity and clarity. She urged entrepreneurs to focus on their core values and how those values translate into their brand. "Your brand is an extension of you," she shared. This perspective shifted how I think about personal and professional branding. From the size of a logo on a pen to its visibility on a billboard, Audrey's expertise illuminated the nuanced art of creating a recognizable and meaningful brand.

Audrey's reflections on mentorship were equally inspiring. "People from the outside can see better or clearer who you are or your potential," she noted. Her experience in a leadership program highlighted the transformative power of guidance and outside perspectives. It was a powerful reminder that seeking support is not a weakness but a strength.

One of the most exciting parts of our conversation was Audrey's vision for 2025—a year she plans to dedicate to relaunching her entrepreneurial career full-time. With a virtual entrepreneur summit planned for each quarter, Audrey is planting seeds for what promises to be an impactful year. Her focus on celebrating progress and using time wisely was a lesson in balancing ambition with intentionality.

Audrey's advice for those starting a business, podcast, or creative project was both practical and inspiring: Define your purpose, be clear on who you want to serve and why. Seek excellence, not perfection—start with your best effort and adjust as you go. Surround yourself with support, whether it's a coach, mentor, or peer; the right connections can help you navigate challenges. Stay connected—build relationships beyond transactions, maintaining genuine communication with your audience and clients.

Audrey's final thoughts encapsulated the essence of our conversation: "It's all about connection." From the relationships she builds with her clients to her work empowering creators, Audrey's success is rooted in her ability to foster trust and collaboration. As I reflected on our interview, I felt inspired by Audrey's unwavering commitment to service and growth. Her story is a beacon for entrepreneurs and creators alike—a reminder that belief, vision, and connection are the cornerstones of meaningful success. Audrey Wiggins' journey is a powerful example of how we can all elevate our work and relationships to new heights. Whether you're just starting out or looking to expand your horizons, her wisdom offers a roadmap to creating impact and achieving your goals.

Season 10, Episode 33, aired 12/28/2024
recorded 12/28/24, Cleveland, OH, US / Bavaria, Germany

Connect with Audrey Wiggins: https://www.altogether.biz/
LinkedIn: https://www.linkedin.com/in/audreywiggins

4.2 John McEntire – The Rhythm of Leadership

In this chapter, I'm excited to share the incredible journey of John Taylor McEntire, a man whose life and career span continents, cultures, and transformative ideas. From working in technology transfer at the University of Illinois to embracing Japanese business practices and fostering community-driven leadership, John's story is a testament to the power of intuition, resilience, and the universal puzzle we're all part of. Let's dive into his insights and actionable strategies to inspire your own leadership path.

John's upbringing was anything but ordinary. Growing up in a culturally rich, faith-based household, he was surrounded by Native American foster brothers, exchange students, and refugees. By 22, he had traveled to 19 countries and all 50 U.S. states. "For me, diversity wasn't something to adjust to; it was simply normal," John explained. This foundation set the stage for his lifelong belief that everyone has a unique piece to add to the puzzle of life.

One of John's defining experiences was his time in Japan, where he learned Ringi Seido and Nemawashi, two transformative business practices. John elaborated: "Nemawashi is rooted in Japanese gardening—it means preparing the roots before transplantation. In business, it translates to laying the groundwork for consensus. Ringi Seido, or the circular system, ensures that decisions are collaborative, starting from the ground up. It may take longer, but the execution is seamless." These practices taught John the value of empowering every individual on a team, fostering an inclusive environment where everyone's input drives collective success.

During his tenure at the University of Illinois, John excelled in technology transfer—bridging groundbreaking research with real-world applications. "From GPS to touchscreens, these innovations came from research funded by national governments. My role was to ensure these ideas reached the world as products and services that benefit humanity," he shared.

However, despite his professional achievements, John found himself in a challenging period. His wife's battle with depression led him to confront his own feelings of stagnation. This pivotal moment introduced him to coaching, which he described as "transformational." Through mentorship, John regained his assertiveness, eventually making significant leaps in his career, including a role in Doha, Qatar.

John's early foray into theater offered invaluable lessons on collaboration and leadership. "The theater is a microcosm of society," he explained. "Everyone has a role—from the lead actors to the stagehands. When every part of the machine works in harmony, the result is magic." This philosophy informed John's leadership style, emphasizing the importance of understanding and leveraging the unique talents of each team member.

The Sync System: A Holistic Approach to Leadership Inspired by his diverse experiences, John developed the Sync System: Synchronize Yourself Naturally within your Community. "It's about breaking communication barriers," he said. "From the boardroom to the family room, understanding different languages—literal or cultural—is key to effective leadership."

Harnessing Intuition John's journey has been guided by intuition, a skill he encourages others to cultivate. "Whether it's Nunchi in Korean culture or simply listening to your gut, intuition is a powerful tool. It helps you read the room, adapt to circumstances, and make decisions that align with your purpose," he explained.

Final Thoughts: Embracing a Growth Mindset John's philosophy is clear: "Don't let your education interfere with your education. Embrace experiential learning, cultivate intuition, and seek mentors who can guide you toward your full potential."

As we wrapped up our conversation, John emphasized the importance of thinking outside the box and empowering others to thrive. His journey from a global upbringing to shaping leadership strategies that drive real-world results is an inspiring roadmap for anyone seeking to lead with purpose and impact.

Takeaway for Readers

- Embrace cultural diversity as a strength in leadership.
- Cultivate intuition to guide your decisions and actions.
- Create space for team members to grow and thrive, just like preparing soil for a bonsai.
- Seek mentors and coaches to unlock your potential and overcome challenges.

John's parting words resonate deeply: "We're all part of a bigger puzzle. Let's find our place and empower others to find theirs."

Season 10, Episode 62, aired 1/11/2025
recorded 1/11/2025 , West Richland, WA, US / Germany

Connect with John McEntire: www.mutualprosperity.com
LinkedIn: https://www.linkedin.com/in/johntaylormcentire/

4.3 Aaron Ryan – Building Worlds

Aaron Ryan's voice carried the kind of energy that only a seasoned storyteller could muster, one who had traversed multiple genres and found depth in the world of imagination. From the moment he began recounting his journey, it was clear that creativity wasn't just a pastime; it was a calling. His story unfolded like one of his novels, brimming with insights, emotions, and powerful lessons.

Aaron shared the origin of his storytelling passion—a second-grade assignment that turned into a lifelong pursuit. As he recounted the tale of "The Electric Boy", a childhood creation that surprisingly echoed his later novel, "Forecast", Aaron's words underscored how early sparks of creativity can ignite a lifelong fire.

"Life comes full circle," he mused, revealing how the themes of his early stories mirrored those he explores today. This was a testament to how our formative experiences often guide the paths we carve as adults, even in ways we might not immediately recognize.

The conversation naturally transitioned to Aaron's "Dissonance" series, a post-apocalyptic saga set in a world not too distant from ours. It wasn't just a tale of alien invasion; it was a mirror reflecting humanity's perpetual struggle with unity. "The true enemy is always man," Aaron observed, weaving a thread of timeless wisdom through his fictional narrative. The Gorgons, terrifying alien predators, were an external threat, but it was human disunity that underscored the heart of the story—a message as relevant as ever.

Aaron's process for crafting such compelling worlds? A blend of intuition and flexibility. While some writers meticulously plan, Aaron described himself as a "pantser," allowing the story to grow organically. His characters often take the lead, guiding the narrative toward unforeseen destinations. It's a style that mirrors life's unpredictability, and Aaron embraces it wholeheartedly.

"I let the characters lead me," he explained. "Art imitates life, and life imitates art."

His openness to inspiration extended beyond fiction. When recounting the bedtime story that became "The Ring of Truth", his first children's book, Aaron spoke of storytelling as a tool for connection and teaching. The themes of shame and identity that he addressed in the book were drawn from his parenting philosophy—an intentional effort to affirm his children's worth while addressing behavior.

As we delved into his creative process, Aaron revealed an unconventional but brilliant strategy: he starts with the book cover. Visualizing the finished product serves as his compass, a tangible motivator to fill the pages with meaning and purpose.

The chapter wouldn't be complete without exploring Aaron's mantra: Your focus determines your reality. It was a mantra that had guided him through the highs and lows of his creative career, reminding him—and us—that clarity and intention can manifest the extraordinary.

Aaron's closing thoughts offered a profound reminder: creativity isn't bound by limitations. It's enriched by the courage to embrace vulnerability, the willingness to grieve, and the determination to keep creating. Whether crafting fictional worlds or navigating real-life challenges, Aaron's journey underscored the transformative power of storytelling.

As the interview concluded, it became evident that Aaron's work wasn't merely about writing books—it was about inspiring others to embrace their creativity, confront their fears, and bring their unique stories to life. His message was simple yet profound: within every story lies the power to connect, heal, and transform.

Season 10, Episode 71, aired 1/16/2025
recorded 1/15/25 Seattle, WA, US / Bavaria, Germany

Connect with Aaron Ryan: https://dot.cards/authoraaronryan

Author Aaron Ryan: https://www.authoraaronryan.com
Book series "The End": https://thisisnottheend.com/
The Dissonnance Sage: https://www.dissonancetheseries.com

4.4 Venchele St. Dic – Empathy in Every Word

When I sat down with Venchele Saint Dic, it became immediately clear that she is a powerhouse of inspiration, blending authenticity and intellect with a deep passion for helping others. Her calm yet resolute demeanor carried every word she spoke, and it was impossible not to be drawn into her story.

She started with a simple truth that resonated deeply: "Authenticity matters. Audiences resonate with honesty," Venchele said. "Content must be transparent, especially when working in spaces like public health or writing where lives, experiences, and vulnerabilities are at the forefront."

This was no theoretical musing for Venchele—it was her life's work. As the founder of Pathway Coach Writing, she's committed to helping aspiring authors and businesses share their stories with clarity and confidence. But there's a deeper layer. Venchele's work is informed by her background in public health leadership, a perspective that infuses everything she touches with empathy and purpose. "Public health is about addressing disparities," she explained. "It's not just about data—it's about the stories behind the numbers. That's where the magic happens."

Listening to Venchele, I couldn't help but reflect on how storytelling bridges the technical and the emotional. It connects the data to the human experience. She spoke passionately about her mission to empower those often left out of mainstream narratives: women, people with disabilities, those navigating behavioral health systems. "Important stories are those that are often left untold," she said. "They're the antidote to a world that often prioritizes surface-level content over depth."

I asked her about the challenges of maintaining authenticity in an era dominated by content marketing. Her response was direct: "We need to be disruptors. The focus shouldn't just be on what sells. It should be on what adds value and shows vulnerability. That's where true connection happens."

Our conversation naturally flowed to the intersection of public health and creative writing. On the surface, these might seem like disparate fields, but Venchele illuminated the synergy between them. She shared how her experience in technical writing—grants, reports, case studies—has shaped her ability to craft narratives that are both impactful and relatable. "Public health taught me to be honest, transparent, and data-driven," she said. "But it also taught me how to use stories to make those data points human."

As she spoke, I realized the depth of her insight: every piece of writing, whether it's a memoir or a technical report, holds the potential to transform. It's not just about the words on the page—it's about the intention behind them. "The content must stir emotions," Venchele said. "That's how you inspire action."

Her advice for aspiring authors was equally compelling. "Start small. Journal daily, even if it's just for 10 minutes. Don't judge yourself. Allow your thoughts to flow without the pressure of perfection. Disparate ideas will eventually connect," she assured. "And who knows? That journaling might just become your next book."

What struck me most was her emphasis on rest—a topic often neglected in discussions about productivity. "Your best work can't come from fatigue," she said. "We live in a culture that glorifies hustle, but rest is critical for creativity and growth."

This philosophy extended to her approach to goal-setting. Venchele spoke of aligning her projects with her values, pacing herself, and rejecting the temptation to compare her journey with others. "Your beginning is not someone else's end," she reminded me. "Trust the process, be vulnerable, and everything will fall into place."

As our conversation drew to a close, Venchele shared a mantra that summed up her worldview beautifully: "Life is a revolving door. Stay relevant, stay growing, and connect with those you'd never expect to meet. And remember, you don't have to boil the ocean. It takes a community to change the world."

I left the interview with a renewed sense of purpose. Venchele's words were a powerful reminder that authenticity, vulnerability, and rest aren't just ideals—they're essential ingredients for meaningful work and a fulfilling life.

Season 10, Episode 70, aired 1/15/2025
recorded 10/14/2024 Washington D.C, US / Bavaria, Germany

Connect with Venchele: https://www.linkedin.com/in/venchele-saint-dic-drph-student-mph-baph-70480811/
Website: https://www.pathwaycoachwriting.com/

4.5 Annette Dernick – Create Peace in Business

When I sat down with Annette Dernick, I knew immediately that this was going to be a conversation that would not only inspire but also deeply resonate. Annette, an expert in fostering love and peace within companies, brings a fresh perspective to organizational dynamics. She is not just a speaker, coach, and author—she's a changemaker committed to transforming workplaces into thriving hubs of appreciation and collaboration. Annette's dedication to cultivating peace is rooted in her own life story. During our conversation, she shared a pivotal and deeply personal experience. "I've always known that peace was important to me," she began. But it wasn't until she was diagnosed with complex PTSD, stemming from her parents' experiences during World War II, that she understood the depth of her calling. "In those moments, I realized why peace had always been at the forefront of my life." This realization guided her professional journey, where she witnessed the conflicts and dysfunctions that can pervade corporate environments. "Companies have their own wars," she noted. "But my mission is to help those leaders who want to bring their organizations to a higher level of peace and appreciation." Her work is aimed at fostering a culture that attracts and retains talent—a particularly vital goal in today's competitive labor market. When asked to define a culture of appreciation, Annette was quick to clarify: "It's not about everyone just being nice to each other. It's about recognizing the inherent worth of every individual in the organization." She highlighted the importance of valuing employees for their unique contributions and fostering an environment where conflicts are addressed constructively. "Conflicts aren't the problem," she explained. "The problem is how we address them. When conflicts are resolved in a spirit of appreciation, teams become stronger, more creative, and more aligned."

Annette's insights on the tangible benefits of a peaceful workplace were equally compelling. Companies with such cultures experience lower turnover, fewer sick days, and increased employee engagement. "Employees who feel valued don't just work harder—they work with their hearts," she said.

"That kind of commitment translates directly to business success."

"It all starts with the leader," Annette emphasized. "Leaders are role models, whether they realize it or not. Their attitude sets the tone for the entire organization." Annette shared her concept of "thought hygiene," likening it to a mental shower. "Just as we cleanse our bodies, we must cleanse our thoughts. Are we starting the day with grumpy, negative thoughts, or are we choosing optimism and possibility?" She encourages leaders to reflect on their mindset each morning and consider the ripple effects of their behavior on their teams. Her advice was as actionable as it was profound. "If leaders approach their teams with genuine interest and care, it creates a chain reaction. Employees mirror that energy, and soon you have a workplace built on mutual respect and collaboration." Throughout our conversation, Annette shared simple yet powerful tools to foster a culture of peace. One of her favorites is the use of "I statements" for addressing issues. For example, instead of saying, "You're always late," a leader might say, "I noticed it was 9:05 this morning. It's important to me that we're ready for our customers by 9." Another technique she recommends is asking open-ended questions to encourage problem-solving. "Instead of saying, 'We can't do this,' ask, 'How can we make this work?'" These simple shifts in language can transform communication and create a more collaborative environment. Annette also emphasized the importance of bringing diverse perspectives into the conversation. "In international teams, each culture brings its own unique strengths. When we approach these differences with curiosity instead of judgment, it leads to innovation and growth." Annette shared a compelling success story of a company that had been struggling with low morale and high conflict. By working with the CEO to clarify expectations and create a more inclusive environment, the company experienced a dramatic turnaround. Employees became more engaged, conflicts were resolved more effectively, and overall productivity soared. "It's not just about making employees happy," she said. "It's about creating a business that thrives. When employees feel valued, they bring their best selves to work. That's good for everyone—the employees, the customers, and the bottom line." As our conversation drew to a close, Annette shared her vision for the future. "I want to reach even more people with this message," she said. "Whether it's through speaking engagements, my book, or one-on-one coaching, my goal is to inspire as many leaders as possible to embrace peace and appreciation in their organizations."

She also revealed plans to publish an English version of her book, The Peace Factor, and to expand her speaking engagements globally. "This is more than a mission for me," she said. "It's a movement. And I believe that together, we can create a world where businesses are a force for good."

Annette left us with a powerful reminder: "Peace begins with you. It starts with the choices you make every day—the thoughts you think, the words you speak, and the actions you take. When you embody peace, you inspire others to do the same. And that's how we change the world."

I couldn't agree more. Annette's message is a call to action for all of us to bring more love, appreciation, and understanding into our workplaces and our lives. And in doing so, we not only transform our businesses—we transform ourselves.

Season 8, Episode 17, aired 10/1/2024
recorded 8/27/24, Bruehl, Germany / Bavaria, Germany

Connect with Annette and **Love & Peace in Companies**:
https://annettedernick.com/kickstart/english

Book "The Peace Faktor" (German): https://amzn.to/40HButh

4.6 Lorna Gale – Coming Home to Self

Caroline Biesalski introduces Lorna Gale as a remarkable guest whose mission is to guide individuals toward living sexually free and spiritually whole. Lorna, a sex and spirit alchemist of the feminine-led life, combines her expertise as an intuitive energy healer, somatic sexologist, and award-winning speaker to create transformative journeys for her clients. Her work revolves around helping people feel at home in their bodies, live empowered lives, and embrace their authentic selves.

Lorna shares her unique journey, reflecting on her upbringing in a religious household where the notion of "saving yourself for marriage" instilled a deep disconnection from her body and sexuality. It wasn't until decades later, after raising her daughters and embarking on her own path of discovery, that Lorna experienced a profound midlife sexual awakening. Through retreats, training, and somatic practices, she reclaimed her identity as a sexual and spiritual being. This awakening not only transformed her personal life but also ignited her professional path.

Lorna emphasizes the interconnectedness of sexuality and spirituality, challenging societal norms that often separate the two. "We come from sex," she says, "the creative force that bridges spirit into the human experience." Her work helps clients tap into this life force energy, recognizing it as the essence of their being. By creating safe and sacred spaces, Lorna guides others to embrace their bodies and release the shame and societal expectations that have kept them disconnected.

Throughout the conversation, Lorna introduces somatic practices, inviting listeners to reconnect with their bodies through conscious breathing and awareness. She encourages tuning into the "body balloon," feeling the breath expand and contract through the torso, back, and even the pelvic bowl, which she describes as the "cauldron of creation." This practice is not just about physical awareness but about anchoring into a state of wholeness and connection.

Lorna draws on her experience as a teacher and intuitive healer, helping people redefine consent—not just as a verbal agreement but as a bodily sensation of alignment. She explains how societal conditioning often overrides our natural boundaries, leading to disconnection and people-pleasing tendencies. Through somatic exercises, she empowers individuals to recognize and honor their inner "yes" and "no," fostering a deeper sense of authenticity and self-trust.

Caroline and Lorna delve into the broader implications of feminine and masculine energies. Lorna redefines femininity and masculinity not as gendered traits but as energy (feminine) and form (masculine). She describes the feminine-led life as one where spirit takes the lead, supported by the masculine, creating harmony and balance. This philosophy underpins her work, allowing individuals to reclaim their wholeness and move beyond societal constructs of gender and sexuality.

As they discuss the spiritual aspects of Lorna's work, she shares her perspective on the Garden of Eden story. Lorna reframes the narrative, suggesting that the offering of the apple symbolizes an awakening to sexual and creative energy. Rather than viewing it as a source of shame, she sees it as an invitation to reclaim our innate divinity and embrace our wholeness. Her insights challenge traditional interpretations, offering a fresh lens through which to view our relationship with sexuality and spirituality.

Caroline expresses deep appreciation for Lorna's wisdom, noting how it aligns with the podcast's theme of inspiration. They discuss the role of mentors and authors in Lorna's journey, including Joseph Kramer, Scott Kiloby, and Robert Scheinfeld, whose work on the power of story deeply resonates with her. Lorna describes life as a "lived story," where every experience, no matter how challenging, holds hidden treasures of growth and transformation.

Lorna's gift for holding space and mirroring others' potential shines throughout the conversation. She highlights the importance of embracing vulnerability and dismantling shame to create a more authentic and joyful life. Her ability to guide others back to their inner truth inspires Caroline and listeners alike.

As the episode concludes, Lorna shares a special offer: a guide titled "6 Benefits to Being Sexually Connected to Your Body" and "1 Powerful Exercise to Support You in That". She encourages listeners to reach out via her website or social media, emphasizing the importance of connection and networking. Caroline echoes this sentiment, reminding the audience to take the opportunity to connect with Lorna and explore the transformative potential of her work.

Season 3, Episode 30, aired 3/7/2024
Season 7, Episode 11, aired 8/13/2024

Connect   with   Lorna:
https://www.trustedbodywork.com/profiles/lorna-gale
LinkedIn: https://www.linkedin.com/in/lorna-gale-b-ed-sse-csb-b52bb75/

4.7 Kimberly Laverdure – Systemize for Success

As Kimberly Laverdure and I began our conversation, I couldn't help but feel the calm strength she radiates. Her presence is both grounded and uplifting, a balance that seemed to mirror her professional ethos. Kimberly, the founder of Systemize for Success, has dedicated her life to helping soul-driven entrepreneurs, coaches, and healers bring harmony to their businesses through streamlined systems and intuitive strategies. What struck me most, though, was how her personal story has shaped her professional mission.

Kimberly's journey began in the corporate world, where she spent 17 years navigating administration and business operations. Life, however, had its own plans. A debilitating injury in 2007 forced her to confront her limitations, leading to years of surgeries, chronic pain, and profound personal challenges. Adding to her trials were the emotional wounds of leaving an abusive marriage and experiencing parental alienation.

But Kimberly didn't let adversity define her. When her sister-in-law's magazine faced an unexpected crisis, Kimberly stepped in. That moment sparked her entry into the online business world. What began as a necessity became her calling, and over the years, she transformed her pain into purpose, creating strategies that help others overcome chaos and reclaim their lives.

Listening to Kimberly describe how she integrates intuitive strategies with cutting-edge technology was fascinating. She spoke about using moon cycles and astrological energy to guide business decisions—a practice I hadn't considered but now find deeply intriguing. "There's a different energy when the moon is waxing or waning," she explained. Her ability to align spiritual intuition with practical tools felt like a modern alchemy—a true testament to her title as a Virtual Life Alchemist.

As she delved deeper into the common mistakes entrepreneurs make, Kimberly's wisdom was undeniable. "Too many platforms or too few," she said, shaking her head. She elaborated on how choosing the wrong tools—or not utilizing them fully—can drain both time and money. Her solution? Thoughtfully selected tech stacks that grow alongside a business, balancing functionality with budget.

Kimberly's passion for feminine leadership was equally inspiring. She emphasized the importance of blending masculine and feminine energies—regardless of gender. "It's about creating an ebb and flow," she said. By embracing intuition and softness alongside structure and action, Kimberly believes businesses can cultivate resilience, harmony, and balance.

Hearing about Kimberly's successes made her advice even more compelling. She shared the story of a former client, a business owner overwhelmed by chaos. Through Kimberly's systems and guidance, he went from constant stress to a state of calm efficiency, finally able to take vacations and enjoy his family. It's stories like these that underline the transformative power of her work.

What impressed me most, though, was Kimberly's humility and her deep commitment to growth. She's not just a teacher— she's a student of life, continuously learning from her mentors, her experiences, and the people she helps. Her future goals, including a group coaching program and a co-authored book, reflect her drive to reach even more people with her message.

As we wrapped up, Kimberly left the audience with a powerful reminder: "Audit your business regularly. You can't always see the inefficiencies when you're inside. And don't forget to reclaim time for yourself—streamline, automate, and live fully."

Kimberly Laverdure embodies what it means to turn challenges into stepping stones. Her story isn't just about survival; it's about thriving and helping others do the same. If you're ready to systemize your business for success, Kimberly's expertise and heart-centered approach might just be the missing piece you've been searching for.

Season 8, Episode 22, aired 10/5/2024
recorded 10/5/2024 Port St Lucie, FL, US / Bavaria, Germany

Connect with Kimberly: https://www.systemizeforsuccess.com
Website: https://virtuallifealchemist.com/
Book „She Defies": https://amzn.to/3WT90KP

4.8 Gillian Sneddon – The Sunshine Effect

Gillian Sneddon's journey is a testament to the transformative power of love, creativity, and determination. As she sat down to share her story, it became clear that her work was born from a deeply personal place—a fusion of heartfelt intention and a desire to make a tangible impact on the world. Gillian's work as an author is anchored in a singular mission: to instill in children a profound sense of love and self-worth, starting at the earliest stages of life.

Her inspiration, as she recounted, came from a deeply intimate source—her son. In the months following his birth, Gillian envisioned a book that could communicate the boundless love she felt for him. What began as a personal project soon evolved into something far greater. Drawing on the teachings of Louise L. Hay, Gillian crafted a book that wasn't merely a bedtime story but a powerful tool for planting seeds of love and affirmation in the minds of children.

At its core, the book is a love letter to the world's children, teaching them they are cherished and adored. Gillian's innovative approach incorporated a mirror within the book, inviting children to look at themselves while reciting affirmations. She believes this simple yet profound exercise has the potential to reshape how children see themselves and their place in the world. This idea, she explained, wasn't only for her son but for all children, particularly those who may have experienced trauma. Her hope is that these words, spoken aloud, become a cornerstone for self-love and resilience.

Gillian's journey to becoming an author wasn't without its challenges. She candidly shared how the process required her to step outside her comfort zone, embracing new skills and tapping into a community of like-minded individuals. She credited her growth to mentors and institutions that have guided her along the way, such as the Napoleon Hill Institute and thought leaders like Bob Proctor and Tony Robbins. These figures not only inspired her but also demonstrated that the pursuit of greatness is within reach for anyone willing to embrace the journey.

Her ability to inspire others extends beyond her book. Gillian emphasized the importance of using her words—whether written or spoken—to uplift those around her. Whether it's a simple "good morning" to a neighbor or a moment of humor shared with a friend, she believes in the ripple effect of kindness and positivity. This philosophy is woven into her daily life, as she consistently seeks ways to brighten the lives of others.

As a creator, Gillian's talents shine in her ability to blend wisdom and compassion into every project she undertakes. Her love for words is evident in her work, from her book to the hypnotherapy recordings she's developed. These recordings, available on platforms like Amazon Music, extend her reach and allow her to help people in deeply personal ways. Creativity, she explained, is her superpower, and it's something she leverages to make a difference in the world.

When discussing goals, Gillian's ambition is both inspiring and grounded in a clear vision. She has set specific targets for her book's reach, aiming to sell millions of copies to touch the lives of as many children as possible. Her larger aspiration is to collaborate with others on creative projects that amplify the message of love and positivity she holds dear.

For Gillian, the act of setting goals is deeply connected to her belief in the power of intention. She shared how the principles of Napoleon Hill and Bob Proctor have shaped her approach, teaching her to visualize success and take actionable steps toward achieving it. Her process of goal-setting is deliberate and measurable, underscoring her commitment to seeing her dreams realized.

When asked how others could support her mission, Gillian's response was simple: connection. She emphasized the value of building relationships and creating a network of support. Her presence on platforms like Facebook and TikTok allows her to share her work and engage with a broader audience. She's also open to collaborations and welcomes opportunities to connect with individuals who share her vision of making the world a more loving place.

Ultimately, Gillian's message is one of love and authenticity. She reminds us all to nurture self-love and to recognize the power we hold in shaping our own lives. Her work is a call to action, encouraging us to embrace our gifts and use them to create positive change. As she continues her journey, Gillian's unwavering belief in the potential for love to transform the world serves as an inspiring example of what's possible when we live with intention and heart.

Season 6, Episode 30, aired 7/19/24
recorded 6/27/24 Scotland, UK / Bavaria, Germany

Connect with Gillian: https://www.linkedin.com/in/gillian-sneddon-bb88302b/
Get the book "Little Ray of Sunshine":
https://www.facebook.com/mylittleray1/?locale=sw_KE&_rdr

4.9 Monique Schmitz – The Power of Choice

There's something profoundly transformative about reconnecting with someone after a year of growth, change, and personal evolution. My two conversations with Monique Schmitz—first in April 2024, then again in February 2025—became a testament to the power of personal transformation, the choices we make, and the undeniable pull of our true potential.

When I first interviewed Monique, I was drawn to her infectious energy, her ability to see the greatness in others before they even recognized it in themselves. She spoke passionately about breaking mental barriers, about the courage it takes to move from point A to point B. At that time, she had just returned from an extended journey through Australia, after having lived in Switzerland and Dubai. She was a living, breathing example of choosing faith over fear.

Her philosophy was simple yet profound: action creates momentum. She didn't just talk about possibilities—she embodied them. In that first interview, she shared how she had overcome limiting beliefs, how she had learned to trust her inner voice, and how she was using her experiences to help others. I remember feeling inspired just listening to her. "The start is what stops most people," she had said, echoing a truth that resonated deeply.

But inspiration, as powerful as it is, must be put into practice. And so, when we reconnected a year later, I was curious—what had changed? Had the fire she carried in 2024 burned even brighter, or had it faded under the weight of new challenges?

As soon as we began our second conversation, I had my answer.

Monique was still the same bold, insightful force, but something had deepened. Her words carried an even stronger sense of certainty. She had taken the principles she preached and applied them in ways that reshaped her life and the lives of those she coached. What struck me most was her clarity—she no longer spoke of breaking through barriers as a goal, but as a way of life.

She had built something remarkable over the past year. Her work had expanded beyond one-on-one coaching into a larger movement—group mentorship programs, immersive events, and mastermind communities designed to empower even more people. She has embraced Australia as her long-term home and has applied for permanent residency — an exciting step toward making her dream a reality.

The phrase that defined our second conversation was "Choose faith or fear." In our first interview, she had touched on this idea, but now she lived it with unwavering conviction. She reminded me that faith and fear exist in the same invisible space—the only difference is which one we lean into.

Perhaps the most profound moment of our second interview was when she described a simple yet transformative exercise: pausing anxiety for three days. Instead of reacting with worry, she encouraged people to stop and consciously seek the good in any situation. "What if," she said, "this isn't a bad thing? What if it's leading you somewhere better?"

Monique shared this powerful insight from Mary Morrissey—the law of nonresistance and the practice of pausing anxiety for three days to consciously look for the good in any situation. Monique finds this approach transformative, using it in her own coaching to help clients shift from fear to possibility. Rather than resisting challenges, she encourages embracing them with curiosity, trusting that clarity and solutions will emerge.

I could feel the depth of her wisdom, a wisdom shaped by experience, persistence, and an unshakable belief in human potential.

Looking back at both conversations, I saw the bridge that connected them: Monique's journey wasn't just about achieving personal success. It was about creating a ripple effect—guiding others to step into their own power, to rewrite their stories, to see that they too had a choice.

And that's the lesson I take away from our time together. Growth isn't about one grand moment of clarity—it's about choosing, every day, to step forward in faith rather than retreat in fear. It's about recognizing that we are not stuck in our circumstances, but rather, we are the architects of our lives.

As Monique put it so perfectly: "The world needs us to step up and be a better version of who we are today."

And what a difference a year can make.

Season 4, Episode 20, aired 4/10/2024
Season 11, Episode 43, aired 2/15/2025

Connect with Monique:
https://www.linkedin.com/in/mjmschmitz/

4.10 Angela Sidlo – The Power of Connection

If you've ever thought about energy, healing, and the power of connection, you're going to want to read this. I sat down with Angela Sidlo, a holistic health expert who's not just talking about wellness—she's changing the game. Angela is a certified reflexologist, aromatherapist, and published author, and her expertise in AcuAroma therapy is making waves worldwide.

We started our conversation with an instant energy shift. You know that moment when you meet someone, and you just *get it?* That's what happened. From the beginning, Angela wasn't just answering my questions—she was inviting me into a whole new perspective on health, energy, and personal empowerment.

The first thing that stood out? She's not just using essential oils for relaxation. She's using them to shift energy at a deep level. And here's where it gets interesting. When an essential oil is distilled, Angela explains, the plant is giving up its life force energy. This isn't just about scent or relaxation—it's about tapping into the actual frequency of the plant and how it interacts with our own body's energy system. The oils communicate with us, and they do it through acupuncture points. It's called AcuAroma therapy, and it's next-level powerful.

And here's where most people get it wrong. They think of essential oils as just a nice-smelling add-on to their self-care routine. They don't realize that there's a science and an energy system behind how these oils interact with the body. Angela is changing that. She's educating people on how to use essential oils strategically—to release blockages, balance emotions, and even rewire subconscious patterns.

I had to ask, *What got you into this work?* Because let's be honest, not everyone wakes up one day and decides to pioneer a whole new approach to healing. Her answer? It started with a personal journey, like most great discoveries do. She wanted to understand not just how we heal, but why we get stuck in the first place. Why do people struggle with the same emotional patterns? Why do they feel blocked? And more importantly—how do they break free?

That's what led her to the work she does today. She's not just helping people feel better; she's giving them tools to take control of their energy, their mindset, and their life.

Now, let's talk about something that really stood out in this interview: connection. Angela's mission isn't just about individual healing. It's about creating circles of connection—learning circles, to be specific. She wants to build a global network of healers, empowering them with the knowledge to transform not only their own lives but the lives of their communities. And she's already doing it. Her card decks are in 12 countries, and her AcuAroma certification program is growing fast.

This is how real transformation happens. It's not just about *one* person making a change. It's about an entire network of people stepping into their power, sharing knowledge, and raising the vibration of the planet together.

And if you're reading this and wondering, *How does this apply to me?*—here's the answer. If you've ever felt stuck, drained, or disconnected, it's not just in your head. It's energy. And the good news? You can shift it.

Angela explained how nature itself works in a network of energy and communication, and the human body is no different. Think of the mycelium network—the way fungi connect underground, sending messages and nutrients across massive distances. Trees in a forest do the same thing. They communicate. They protect each other. They share resources.

Humans are meant to do the same. We thrive in connection.

This is why Angela is creating these circles—because just like the trees, just like the mycelium, we are stronger when we support each other. And when we actively raise our energy, when we surround ourselves with the right people, when we tap into the frequencies that lift us up instead of hold us down— we change.

Now, I know what you're thinking. *This all sounds great, but how do I actually use this?*

Angela's answer is simple: start small, but start intentionally.

A smile. Yes, a smile is energy. It's an invitation to connection, a way of telling the world, *I'm open. I'm here. I see you.* It's one of the simplest ways to shift energy instantly.

But beyond that? It's about creating a practice. Surround yourself with high-vibration people. Learn to use essential oils in a strategic way—not just for scent, but for actual energy work. And most importantly, step into learning and connection.

Angela's goal is to certify as many people as possible in her AcuAroma therapy method, so they can start their own learning circles, help their communities, and become part of this global movement. And right now, she's offering 50% off her Level 1 certification, which includes training, a consultation, and resources to get started.

If you've ever wanted to understand how energy works, how to break through emotional and mental roadblocks, or even how to build a purpose-driven business in holistic health, this is it. You already have everything you need to step into your next level. The question is, are you ready to make the shift?

Season 4, Episode 25, aired 4/14/2024
recorded 3/23/24 Gearhart, OR, US / Bavaria, Germany
Connect with Angela: http://www.learnangelasidlo.com/

4.11 John Verrico – The Fire within

John Verrico's journey was never a straight path. As a young boy, he was small, an easy target for bullies. He felt insignificant, unseen, and without much to offer. The world seemed to be divided into two groups—those who took up space and those who faded into the background. And for a long time, John believed he belonged to the second group.

But everything changed when he discovered something unexpected—disco dancing. What began as a personal mission to build confidence became a turning point that shaped the rest of his life.

John had spent years watching from the sidelines as others took center stage. At school dances, and later in night clubs, he saw how those who could move effortlessly on the floor seemed to hold a certain power, a magnetism that drew people in. He envied them and wanted those same abilities.

So, he studied. He watched "American Bandstand" and "Soul Train," analyzing every step, every turn, every shift of weight. He practiced relentlessly, pushing himself to master the moves. He even created some of his own unique moves. And then, when he was ready, he stepped onto the dance floor.

The first time he danced in public, something incredible happened. People noticed him—not for his size, not for his weaknesses, but for his skill. The very thing that had made him feel invisible was gone, replaced by a new sense of confidence.

Soon, he wasn't just dancing—he was teaching. Others wanted to learn from him, to experience the same confidence that movement gave him. And in helping them, he found something even more valuable than skill—he found purpose.

This moment of discovery was more than just about dance; it was about realizing that value doesn't come from being the biggest, the loudest, or the most naturally gifted. Value comes from what you cultivate within yourself and share with others.

That same purpose has guided John throughout his diverse career, from janitor to comedian, Navy Master Chief to public affairs leader, and now, as a speaker and mentor. No matter the role, his mission remained the same: to help others see their worth.

As he moved through different professions, John noticed a pattern—too many people didn't recognize their own potential. They underestimated what they had to offer and often let the world tell them their limits. He understood this feeling all too well.

He also saw that leadership was often misunderstood. Many people assumed that to be a leader meant being the loudest voice in the room, the one in control, the one calling the shots. But John believed leadership wasn't about standing above others; it was about lifting them up.

He saw firsthand how people in all walks of life wanted the same things—to be trusted, respected, and given opportunities. And he realized that when people felt valued, they thrived. This understanding became the foundation of everything he did, leading him to develop a framework based on five essential elements: **Trust, Opportunity, Respect, Communication, and Humanity—TORCH.**

"These five things," John explains, "are what every person needs to truly shine. And when you light someone else's torch, the world gets brighter for both of us."

John's philosophy wasn't just theory; it was something he lived by. Whether in the military, the corporate world, government agencies, or on stage as a speaker, he made it his mission to elevate others.

"You don't have to put out someone else's flame to make yours burn brighter," John says. "The more we allow others to shine, the more we light up the world together."

This lesson became his life's work. From the dance floor to the Navy and government service to public speaking, John has dedicated himself to showing others their worth, their power, and their ability to thrive despite obstacles. The world can be dark at times, filled with division, fear, and uncertainty, but the solution isn't to retreat into that darkness—it's to light the way.

Through his career in public affairs, John worked with countless individuals who struggled with self-doubt, many of whom had powerful talents and ideas but held themselves back. He would often tell them:

"You already have the fire inside of you. You just need to share it."

And time after time, he saw what happened when people embraced their own power. The moment they realized they had something valuable to give, their confidence skyrocketed.

John believes that everyone, no matter their background, has a gift to offer the world. And that gift isn't about personal success—it's about contribution. It's about making a difference in the lives of others. Looking back, he sees now that the bullying he endured as a child taught him one of the most profound lessons of his life: that he could choose how to respond. He could let it define him, or he could take control of his own story. He chose the latter.

We all have a fire within us. The question is: **will you share yours?**

Season 11, Episode 47, aired 2/17/2025
recorded 1/23/2025 York, PA, US / Bavaria, Germany
Connect with John: https://www.johnverrico.com/

4.12 Katharine Giovanni – Freedom through Forgiveness

As I sat down with Katharine Giovanni, her energy filled the space like sunlight breaking through clouds after a storm. She radiated a kind of wisdom and calm that only comes from someone who has truly walked through fire and come out stronger on the other side. You could feel it in her voice, her words, the way she talked about forgiveness as if it were both a battle and a balm. This wasn't just theory for her—it was life, lived and experienced, with all its jagged edges and soft landings.

Katharine opened up with a bold statement that hung in the air: *"When people hear the word forgiveness, they go straight to their 10. The unforgivable. But that's not where the work begins."* She smiled knowingly, as if she'd just read everyone's mind. "Start small," she said. "Start with the person who cut you off in traffic, the friend who canceled plans last minute, or the coworker who stole your sandwich from the breakroom fridge. Forgiveness doesn't have to start with the big stuff—it's a process."

And as she explained this, it hit me how much we complicate forgiveness. How we make it about the other person—about excusing, forgetting, or somehow letting someone else off the hook. But Katharine flipped that on its head. *"Forgiveness isn't about them,"* she said. *"It's about you. It's selfish in the best possible way. You're clearing out the clutter in your own head, letting go of the anger that's taking up space and energy you could be using for something else. It's about freedom."*

She leaned in closer, as if letting me in on a secret. *"Anger is heavy,"* she continued, picking up her coffee cup and holding it in front of her face. *"It's like holding this cup out in front of you all day. At first, it's fine. You don't even notice it. But over time, your arm starts to hurt, your energy drains, and eventually, that cup becomes all you can focus on. Forgiveness,"* she said, lowering the cup, *"is putting it down. It's freeing yourself from the weight."*

I couldn't help but ask the obvious: "But what about those big moments? The real hurt, the people who did the unforgivable?" Katharine didn't miss a beat. She acknowledged the depth of that pain but offered a fresh perspective. "Sometimes, forgiveness isn't about the person at all. It's about forgiving the energy around the situation, forgiving yourself, forgiving the memories. You don't have to talk to that person. You don't even have to think about them. It's about taking back control of your own story."

And that's what struck me most about Katharine's approach—it wasn't about minimizing pain or pretending things didn't happen. It was about reframing it, taking back your power, and deciding that your future wasn't going to be written by what happened in the past. "Forgiveness isn't forgetting," she emphasized. "It's about remembering without the emotional charge. It's about neutrality."

Her words carried a kind of gravity that made me want to sit back and take stock of my own life. The places I was holding on too tightly, the people and situations that had long since moved on while I still carried their weight. And she wasn't just talking about people. She urged us to forgive places, memories, even objects if they carried bad energy for us. *"It's not just about the who—it's about the what."*

By the end of our conversation, Katharine had me completely rethinking what forgiveness really means. It's not a gift you give to someone else. It's a gift you give yourself. It's a declaration of freedom, a bold step toward becoming the person you were always meant to be. "Forgiveness is what clears the path," she said, smiling softly. *"It lets you stop surviving and start thriving."*

As we wrapped up, I couldn't help but feel an overwhelming sense of gratitude—not just for Katharine's words, but for the way she lived them. Her story, her lessons, her energy—it was all a reminder that we have the power to change the narrative. We can't control what happens to us, but we can control what we do with it. And sometimes, all it takes is the courage to let go.

Season 10, Episode 4, aired 12/13/2024
recorded 10/1/24 Leland, NC, US / Bavaria, Germany

Connect with Katharine: http://www.katharinegiovanni.com/
The Ultimate Path To Forgiveness: https://amzn.to/3AJcqaP

4.13 Dr. Edward Feinberg – Truth in Dentistry

Dr. Edward Feinberg's passion for dentistry is undeniable. His knowledge, expertise, and dedication to preserving and restoring teeth rather than extracting them set him apart in a field increasingly driven by efficiency and economic interests. In our conversation, he shared not just his wisdom but his urgent mission: to educate both dentists and patients about the true principles of long-lasting dental health and the critical importance of making informed decisions.

A second-generation dentist trained by his father, Dr. Elliot Feinberg, Dr. Feinberg has spent decades preserving techniques that have been largely forgotten by modern practitioners. He has documented over 70 years of successful restorative dentistry with more than 100,000 photos—living proof that traditional crown and bridge techniques, when done correctly, can last 30, 40, or even 50 years. And yet, he watches as these proven methods are pushed aside in favor of quick-fix solutions, many of which lack a long-term track record.

One of the most striking points Dr. Feinberg made was about the overuse and often unnecessary application of dental implants. He expressed deep concern that many dentists, lacking confidence in their crown and bridge skills, are too quick to extract teeth and replace them with implants—without fully exploring the possibility of saving the natural tooth. "Patients should understand that just because one dentist told them their teeth can't be saved doesn't mean another can't save them," he emphasized. He encouraged people to seek second opinions, just as they would for a major medical diagnosis, rather than blindly accepting the first recommendation given to them.

This message is not just about preserving teeth—it's about **empowering patients**. Dr. Feinberg strongly believes that people should not feel pressured into drastic dental treatments without fully understanding their options. "Dentistry is rarely an emergency," he explained. "You have time to ask questions, to seek other opinions, and to make a decision that is truly right for you." His perspective calls for a shift in the patient-dentist relationship—one where patients are active participants, armed with knowledge rather than passive recipients of treatment plans they don't fully understand.

Beyond patient education, Dr. Feinberg is also on a mission to **reshape the way dentistry is taught and practiced**. His online platform, Onward, is a continuation of the legacy started by his father in 1957, offering in-depth training on full-coverage restorative dentistry. He wants to ensure that today's dentists are equipped with the skills necessary to preserve teeth whenever possible, rather than defaulting to extraction and implants. Yet, he acknowledges the challenges: modern dental students often graduate with immense debt, leading them to prioritize high-production workflows over quality patient care. This, he argues, is fundamentally at odds with the principles of longevity and health that should be at the core of dentistry.

Dr. Feinberg's work is **a call to action**—for both dentists and patients. For dentists, it's a challenge to uphold the highest standards of care, to seek out knowledge beyond what they learned in school, and to prioritize patient health over financial incentives. For patients, it's an invitation to **take control of their dental health**, to ask questions, and to never assume that extraction is the only option.

As our conversation wrapped up, Dr. Feinberg left us with a simple but powerful message: **"Don't rush. Get informed. Seek a second opinion. And make choices that are truly in your best interest."** These words extend far beyond dentistry—they are a reminder to approach all aspects of life with curiosity, patience, and the courage to make choices that align with our well-being.

For those who want to learn more, Dr. Feinberg's book *Open Wide* and his online platform **The Onward Program** offer deep insights into these topics. His mission is not just about preserving teeth—it's about **preserving knowledge,**

integrity, and the right for every patient to make fully informed decisions about their health.

Season 11, Episode 24, aired 2/5/2025
recorded 10/24/24 Scarsdale, NY, US / Bavaria, Germany

Connect with Dr. Edward Feinberg:
https://www.linkedin.com/in/edward-feinberg-b79b2a15

4.14 Liliana Cavaliere Hintz – Recipe for Success

In this chapter of *The Inspired Choice Chronicles*, I had the pleasure of speaking with Liliana Cavaliere Hintz, a woman whose journey embodies resilience, transformation, and the power of inspired action. Our conversation was a deep dive into self-discovery, leadership, and the principles of success that have shaped her life.

Liliana's story begins in Italy, where she was born and raised before making a life-changing move to the United States at 24. Her journey, however, was not just geographical—it was a transformation of mindset, ambition, and purpose. She built a life in a new country, learned a new language, and, over time, became a successful business owner in the restaurant industry. But what truly shaped her path were the teachings of Napoleon Hill, Earl Nightingale, and Bob Proctor—mentors whose philosophies of personal development and success guided her every step.

For nearly four decades, Liliana ran her own restaurant, but in reality, she was doing much more than serving meals—she was coaching. She understood that leadership wasn't just about giving instructions but about inspiring people to see the best in themselves. The success of her restaurant was no accident; it was built on the same principles she teaches today:

Empowerment through belief – Helping employees see their own potential

Long-term vision – Leading with purpose and persistence

Giving to receive – Understanding that contribution fuels success

Her approach led to unheard-of employee retention in the restaurant industry—staff members stayed for 20+ years, a testament to the deep impact she had on their personal and professional growth.

One of the most powerful moments in our conversation was when Liliana shared a key insight about decision-making:

"Success doesn't happen overnight. First, you decide that you're going to have success. Then, everything else follows."

This philosophy carried her through major transitions, including selling her restaurant just weeks before the pandemic hit, a decision that could easily be seen as fate, luck, or—as Liliana believes—a manifestation of clear intention and aligned action.

Now, Liliana dedicates her time to coaching others, helping them uncover their true desires, purpose, and potential. She works with clients through Thinking Into Results (TIR), the transformational program developed by Bob Proctor, designed to break limiting beliefs and create lasting success.

For those new to self-development, she also offers a one-month teaser program, a gentle but powerful introduction to the principles that can awaken the inner child and reignite curiosity about life's possibilities.

Her heart-centered approach is what sets her apart—she believes in one-on-one coaching, ensuring a deep, personal connection with each client.

For those interested in working with Liliana, she offers an exclusive opportunity: Mention the code "INSPIRED" and receive a special offer on her coaching programs!

Liliana teaches both in English and Italian, making her programs accessible to an even wider audience. Whether you are looking to break free from limitations, gain clarity on your goals, or simply be inspired by someone who has walked the path, Liliana is a mentor who leads with wisdom, experience, and heart.

Liliana's journey is a testament to the power of belief, resilience, and inspired action. She reminds us that success is not about where you start but about the choices you make along the way.

"You tell me what you want, and I'll show you how to get it."

This is more than a promise—it's a philosophy that has guided her life and now helps transform the lives of others.

I encourage you to reach out to Liliana—her wisdom, warmth, and experience are truly inspiring.

Season 2, Episode 4, aired 12/28/2023
recorded 12/27/23 Florida US / Bavaria, Germany

Connect with Liliana: https://www.linkedin.com/in/liliana-cavaliere-hintz-478b7236/

4.15 Brian Elam – The Power of Network

If you're an entrepreneur, you've probably heard the phrase, *"Your network is your net worth."* But how many of us truly understand what that means? In my conversation with Brian Elam, host of *Get Your Entrepreneurship Together* podcast, we dug deep into this concept—and let me tell you, Brian didn't hold back. Brian has seen firsthand how building the right network can make or break a business. Early in his journey, he learned the hard way that no matter how great your idea is, without people, partnerships, and connections, success remains out of reach. And if you're stuck in a cycle of *doing it all alone*, this chapter is for you. Brian's first business was what he thought was a brilliant idea—a platform like Angie's List for natural health care providers. It had all the makings of a great startup: a solid concept, an in-demand service, and the tech to back it up. But there was just one problem: he was doing it alone.

"I was focused inside the business instead of on it," he admitted. He didn't ask himself the right questions:

Who do I need to talk to who has done this before? Who has the experience I can learn from? How can I bring others into my vision?

Had he built the right network and mentorship circle, things could have turned out very differently. Most business owners make the mistake of trying to do everything themselves—not realizing that alignment is the real key to success. Brian broke it down like this:

You have skills and strengths—focus on those. You have weaknesses—delegate or automate them. If you're stuck doing things that drain you, your business is stuck too.

Whether you're a solopreneur or leading a growing team, recognizing what you *shouldn't* be doing is just as important as knowing what you *should*. If a task doesn't align with your passion and skill set, it's time to find someone—or something—that can do it for you.

Another game-changer? Setting boundaries.

Most of us struggle with saying no because we worry about how we'll be perceived. But Brian had a powerful reframe:

"Saying no doesn't make you a bad person. It makes people respect you more. When you finally say yes, they know you mean it."

By defining your priorities—business, family, health, personal growth—you can create non-negotiable time blocks. This helps you focus on what truly matters while avoiding distractions that drain your energy.

One of the most mind-blowing takeaways from our conversation was Brian's perspective on success. Too many people chase an *external* version of success—money, status, a fancy car—without asking themselves:

"What does success actually mean to ME?"

For some, it's a mansion and a Ferrari.
For others, it's a simple home, financial security, and time freedom.
For Brian, it's the ability to walk on the beach in the middle of the day without being tied to his business 24/7.

Your definition of success should be yours alone—not society's, not Instagram's, not someone else's dream.

Brian is confident that small businesses will dominate the market over the next decade. Yes, big corporations will still exist, but the power will shift toward individual entrepreneurs and small business owners.

And here's why that's exciting:

More good people making money = more good happening in the world. Small business owners understand real problems and can create real solutions. Local and online entrepreneurs will drive positive change in communities worldwide.

Brian left us with a final, powerful insight:

"Find what lights you up. Align your business with that passion. If you do, nothing can stop you."

If you've been struggling with feeling stuck, overworked, or unclear on your next step, this is your wake-up call. Success isn't about working harder—it's about working smarter, surrounding yourself with the right people, and staying aligned with your purpose.

Now it's your turn: What's one thing you can delegate or automate today to get back into alignment?

And don't forget: Your network is your net worth. Start building yours today.

Season 11, Episode 59, aired 2/23/2025
recorded 2/22/25 Phoenix, AZ, US / Bavaria, Germany

Connect with Brian: https://www.linkedin.com/in/brianpelam/

4.16 Marie Öholm – The Queen's awakening

"Hello, and welcome, Inspired Podcast community. This is your new episode." I began, my voice steady with excitement as I introduced the day's transformative conversation. Today, I had the privilege of interviewing Marie Öholm—a woman whose journey from relentless workaholism to embracing the full spectrum of her feminine power is as inspiring as it is authentic.

Marie's story is one of radical awakening. Once trapped in a cycle of overwork and a toxic blend of masculine and feminine energies, she described a moment of profound clarity—a moment when, as she vividly recalled, a lifetime of repressed emotions exploded like a burst of unsweetened, bitter Coca-Cola. That explosion, painful yet liberating, marked the beginning of her transformation. No longer defined by control, anger, or the relentless need to please, Marie chose to honor her vulnerability and authenticity.

Her journey wasn't just about letting go of the past—it was about reclaiming her inherent worth. As she shared, "I was living in a codependency, caught in a cycle of toxic energies. But four years ago, I woke up and realized that everything I needed was already inside me." This powerful shift led her to step into what she now calls "queen formation," a way of living that celebrates every facet of one's being.

Throughout our conversation, Marie emphasized the importance of connection—both with oneself and with others. One of her greatest gifts is her ability to truly listen. In every interaction, she creates a safe space where vulnerability is met with compassion and tough love in equal measure. "I want to be as authentic as possible," she said, acknowledging that her journey isn't about presenting a flawless exterior, but about embracing life's imperfections.

She recounted small, everyday moments that fueled her inspiration. Whether it was sharing a smile with a bathroom cleaner at an airport or exchanging a kind word with a stranger,

Marie believes that true connection is built on the simplest acts of recognition and gratitude. These moments, often overlooked, remind us that every person has a story worth hearing and that our shared human experience is filled with opportunities for growth and joy.

In our discussion about setting goals for the future, Marie's pragmatic approach shone through. She balances her visionary ideas with clear, actionable steps. For 2025, she has set both long-term and short-term goals—her current mission being to guide 150 women on a transformational journey through her new signature program. It's a goal born from her own evolution, a way to extend the wisdom of her past to those ready to step into their own power.

Marie's method is simple yet profound: "Every decision, every step, must serve the goal of aligning with who we truly are. I always ask myself, 'Does this choice move me toward my true mission, or does it keep me stuck in the past?'" This clarity of purpose, she explains, is what allows her—and anyone willing to embrace it—to keep moving forward, even in the face of life's inevitable challenges.

What truly sets Marie apart is her commitment to authenticity. In a world where perfection is often mistaken for strength, she chooses to reveal the reality behind the polished surface. "I have days when I'm not 100%—when I feel the weight of a virus or the sting of vulnerability—but that's still me," she admitted with a smile. For Marie, authenticity is the cornerstone of true empowerment. It's about shedding the layers of societal expectations and allowing one's genuine self to shine.

Her approach is a refreshing reminder that inspiration is not about projecting an image of infallibility. Instead, it's about connecting deeply with others by sharing our struggles, our triumphs, and the messy in-between. As Marie put it, "We all have a queen within us, waiting to be acknowledged and celebrated. My mission is to help every woman discover that truth."

Our conversation concluded on a note that resonated deeply with me—a reminder of the power of self-worth. Marie shared one of her favorite quotes from Brené Brown: "Why are we all hustling so hard for our worthiness when all we have to do is claim it?" It's a call to action for every listener to double down on their self-belief, to understand that our perceived limitations are often self-imposed. "Your worthiness," she said, "is the ceiling of your life's experience. Claim it, and watch as your world transforms."

As I wrapped up the interview, I couldn't help but feel that Marie's story was not just about her own evolution—it was a beacon for anyone ready to break free from limiting beliefs and embrace the beauty of their true self. In every word she shared, there was a forward-thinking promise: that by daring to be real, we can all become the queens of our own lives.

So, dear Inspired Podcast community, as you reflect on today's conversation, I invite you to look within. Recognize the queen that resides in you, and know that every small act of self-love and authenticity paves the way for a more empowered tomorrow.

Until next time—keep shining, keep growing, and never stop choosing the inspired path ahead.

Season 5, Episode 41, aired 6/13/2024
recorded 5/8/24 Sweden / Bavaria, Germany

Connect with Marie: https://www.linkedin.com/in/marie-öholm-15243113/

4.17 Norman Gräter – See Life Differently

From the moment I sat down with Norman Gräter, I knew this conversation would be different. Norman isn't just a speaker or an author—he's a force of nature, a walking embodiment of inspiration. As he introduced himself as "the Inspirator," it wasn't just a title; it was a declaration of purpose. His energy, his passion, and his deep belief in personal transformation filled the conversation with an electric charge. And as we talked, I realized that Norman doesn't just teach personal growth—he lives it.

Our journey together began in the most serendipitous way— through Clubhouse, TikTok, and even an English reading group. We met in person in Ottawa, Amsterdam, and even on a cruise ship, yet every encounter felt like another chapter in a larger story of connection and synchronicity. Norman's love for books and learning, particularly the teachings of Neville Goddard and David Hawkins, revealed his insatiable curiosity—his desire not just to know more but to **become more**. He spoke about rereading books and discovering "new" wisdom in them each time, not because the words had changed, but because he had. That insight alone speaks volumes about his journey.

Norman's path has been one of evolution. From being inspired by great minds like Tony Robbins, Esther Hicks, and Joe Dispenza to becoming a transformational leader himself, his shift from commercial self-development to deeper spiritual exploration was clear. But what struck me most was how **he inspires others**. When I asked, his answer was beautifully simple: he listens, he reflects, and he follows his intuition. Whether it's through his keynotes, his writing, or his unique "blue glasses" perspective, Norman invites people to **see life through a lens of joy, possibility, and purpose**.

One of his greatest talents, he shared, is knowing exactly how to refine a story to make it touch people's hearts. He doesn't just tell stories—he **emotionalizes** them, ensuring they

move people, not just inform them. That's his magic. As he described his role in helping others craft impactful speeches, I realized that Norman isn't just about sharing ideas—he's about transformation. And it's not just talk. I've **seen** him do this, live on stage, where his energy, presence, and storytelling create moments so powerful they bring people to tears—tears of realization, release, and sometimes, joy.

But Norman's story doesn't stop with speaking. His latest venture? A **movie project** based on his life, *I Am Gräter*, already endorsed by industry heavyweights. He's not just dreaming about impact—he's making it happen. His unwavering belief in his vision is a lesson in itself: **when you own your greatness, the world responds.**

Norman left us with one profound reminder: **"You don't need to be a copy of anyone. Be yourself, be true, and you will be greater."** In a world that often pressures us to fit in, his message is a call to stand out—not by force, but by authenticity. And that, more than anything, is what makes Norman Gräter truly inspiring.

About Norman Gräter – The Inspirator

Award-winning motivational speaker, C-level consultant, and author. Norman has interviewed over 400 celebrities about their success secrets, inspiring people worldwide to unlock their potential.

Season 1, Episode 21, aired 12/18/2023
recorded 12/18/23 Berlin, Germany / Echo Park, LA, USA

Connect with Norman:
https://beyourself-academy.com/en/home/

4.18 Dr. Denise Brown – The Fairy God Doctor

Interviewing Dr. Denise Brown was a transformative experience that reshaped the way I think about possibility and personal power. From the very beginning, Denise's authenticity and humor set the tone for a conversation that was both deeply personal and universally applicable. As she spoke about the toxic nature of the word "should," she explained that it carries with it a weight of external judgment that forces us to second-guess our choices. Instead of being trapped by "should," she encouraged us to consider what we "could" do—what we truly desire, whether it's the kind of career we want, the love we deserve, or the life we aspire to live. Her message was simple yet revolutionary: remove the limitations imposed by expectations, and open up a space where every decision becomes a bold step towards a life designed on our own terms.

Denise's journey is as compelling as her insights. A Stanford-trained physician, executive, and devoted mom, she has long been known as the fairy god doctor—a title that captures her unique blend of professional expertise and maternal warmth. In our conversation, she recounted how the seeds of her transformative approach were planted early in her life. Despite being a mom to two boys, Denise found a way to nurture a different kind of family by embracing women she affectionately calls her fairy goddaughters. Over the years, these relationships evolved into intimate mentoring sessions where questions about balancing a high-powered career with personal fulfillment were laid bare. Denise revealed that whether her fairy goddaughters were in their twenties, thirties, or even forties, they all grappled with the same internal conflict: the tension between achieving professional success and maintaining a rich, fulfilling personal life.

Her candidness about personal loss added a powerful layer to our dialogue. Denise shared that when she was 24, she experienced the profound grief of losing her mother unexpectedly—a moment that shattered her world but ultimately became a catalyst for change. Instead of allowing the pain to paralyze her, she embraced the loss as a gift. It taught her the harsh reality that life is too short to be spent in constant worry about meeting others' expectations. This painful lesson propelled her into a space where she could make courageous, sometimes unconventional decisions without the crippling fear of failure. "The worst thing that ever happened to you often turns out to be a great gift," she stated, encapsulating her philosophy that every setback carries the seeds of future opportunity.

Denise's approach to decision-making is refreshingly pragmatic. Drawing on her extensive experience as a physician, she explained that making decisions is not about burning bridges or eliminating all alternatives. Instead, it's about gathering the necessary information, making the best choice available at that moment, and then remaining open to change as new insights emerge. This philosophy resonated with me because it challenges the common notion that every decision must be perfect and irreversible. In her words, "You make the best choice you can at the moment you need to make it, and then you get more information and you do it differently." This fluidity in decision-making, she argued, is what allows us to lead dynamic, fulfilling lives without being burdened by regret or the fear of making mistakes.

One of the most memorable parts of our conversation was when Denise recounted a transformative moment with a friend she calls Miss R. Miss R had a string of relationships that were more about the thrill of drama than genuine care. At a yoga retreat, during a moment of vulnerability, Miss R received a bouquet of flowers—a simple gesture that spoke volumes. Denise humorously dubbed them the "F me flowers," a playful yet pointed reminder that if you can't appreciate genuine kindness, you deserve nothing less. The story was a perfect illustration of Denise's belief that sometimes it takes a dose of irreverence and humor to break through long-held patterns of self-doubt and unworthiness. By reframing the situation with light-hearted candor, Miss R was able to see her value clearly and eventually embraced the love and care she deserved. This anecdote not only exemplified Denise's ability to transform challenging situations into opportunities for growth but also underscored the importance of being open to both inspiration and new information.

Throughout our dialogue, it was evident that Denise's mission is not just about achieving success, but about creating a rich tapestry of life where every moment counts. She emphasized that life is a series of choices and that each decision, no matter how small, contributes to the larger picture of who we are. Her advice was both empowering and pragmatic: be deliberate with your words, be bold in your choices, and remember that every decision is reversible except for the moments that truly define us. This perspective was particularly striking because it liberates us from the paralyzing fear of making the "wrong" choice and instead invites us to see every decision as a step towards a more vibrant life.

As our conversation drew to a close, Denise shared her vision for the future—a future where people embrace their ability to choose courageously, where communities are built on genuine connections, and where success is measured not by external standards but by the fulfillment of our own dreams. She spoke passionately about her work mentoring founders and CEOs, and about her commitment to guiding her fairy goddaughters through the complexities of modern life. Her vision is one of inclusivity, resilience, and relentless pursuit of what truly matters.

The conversation was a blend of laughter, heartfelt stories, and practical strategies—a true reflection of Denise's multifaceted approach to life. It wasn't just about the decisions we make; it was about understanding the language we use to frame those decisions.

Season 12, Episode 55, aired 4/5/2025
recorded 2/24/2025 Austin, TX, US / Bavaria, Germany

Connect with Dr. Denise: https://www.denisesbrownmd.com/

5. BECOMING A DREAM GUEST

Being a guest on a podcast is more than just showing up—it's about making a lasting impression and creating real value for both the host and the audience. After recording over 700 interviews in just 14 months, I've seen firsthand what sets *extraordinary guests* apart. The best ones bring authenticity, engagement, and generosity, rather than just promoting themselves.

A great guest stands out from the crowd by being punctual, showing genuine interest in the host's work, and taking time to prepare. Before the interview, take these steps:

1. Research the podcast – Listen to at least one or two previous episodes to understand the host's style and audience.
2. Follow the host on social media – Engage with their posts, share their content, and get familiar with their messaging.
3. Send an ebook or valuable resource – This helps the host prepare thoughtful questions and adds value to the audience.

Most importantly, think about what you can give before you take. If you show up with a spirit of contribution, you'll instantly stand out as a dream guest.

Your energy and engagement will make or break the conversation. The best guests:

- Ask the host questions too – Show interest in their work and mission.
- Keep answers concise yet meaningful – No one wants a monologue.
- Speak with enthusiasm – A warm, engaged tone keeps the audience hooked.

Your role as a guest doesn't end when the recording stops. Here's how you can make a lasting impression:

- Send a thank-you message – A simple follow-up email or DM goes a long way.
- Share the episode – Promote it across all your platforms, tagging the host.
- Introduce the host to others – If you know someone who would be a great guest for their show, make the connection.

Some guests even go the extra mile by sending handwritten thank-you notes, signed books, or small gifts. These thoughtful gestures leave a lasting impression and often lead to future collaborations.

Being a dream guest isn't about self-promotion—it's about relationship-building. When you prioritize value, engagement, and generosity, you set yourself apart in a crowded space.

And never forget: giving is receiving. When you give in silence you will receive back multiplied.

A podcast interview isn't just a one-time opportunity—it's the start of a potential long-term relationship. Many of my best collaborations have come from guests who approached their interview as a two-way street, not just a promotion opportunity.

One of the best ways to build trust is to offer something before expecting anything in return. This could be:

- A glowing review for the podcast on Apple Podcasts, Spotify, PodMatch, GoodPods or Podchaser.
- A LinkedIn endorsement or recommendation if you connected professionally.
- A social media shoutout—not just for your episode but for the podcast as a whole.

I once had a guest who offered revenue-sharing—he told me, "If listeners from this episode sign up for my service using a code, I'll share a percentage with you." This showed respect for the platform and made the collaboration even more valuable.

A good relationship doesn't end after the podcast. Keep it alive by:

- Engaging with the host's content regularly.
- Inviting them to your platform—whether it's another podcast, an event, or a live discussion.
- Checking in periodically—a simple "Hey, how's everything going?" can go a long way.

One guest once suggested a mutual feedback session, where we both shared thoughts on how the episode went and what we could improve. This deepened our connection and made future interviews even better.

When you view each podcast appearance as a door to a bigger network, the opportunities become limitless.

I also offer each of my guests the opportunity to return in a year for another episode. This fosters accountability, maintains connection, and allows us to track the goals they shared during their first appearance.

If you've been a guest before or would like to be my next inspired interview partner, feel free to reach out! My favorite platform for connecting with guests is PodMatch.

7. MASTERING THE ART OF CONVERSATION

Great podcast conversations don't feel like interviews—they feel like effortless, engaging exchanges. But crafting a conversation that captivates an audience takes more than just answering questions.

Some of the best guests ask questions back to the host. This shifts the dynamic from an interview to a real conversation. Instead of simply answering, try:

- "That's an interesting question. What's your take on that?"
- "I know you've interviewed a lot of guests—who had a similar experience?"
- "Before we move on, I'd love to know—has this topic come up in past episodes?"

This creates a more engaging exchange and keeps the host invested in the conversation.

Listeners can tell when a guest is just waiting for their turn to speak versus when they're truly engaged. The best way to practice active listening is to:

1. Acknowledge what the host says – Build on their thoughts rather than pivoting immediately to your next point.
2. Pause before responding – This prevents rushed, rehearsed answers and allows for deeper, more natural discussions.
3. Emphasize storytelling over facts – People connect more with personal stories and struggles than with stats and figures.

A great conversation isn't about how much you talk, but about how well you connect with the host and audience. Being a dream podcast guest means engaging in meaningful dialogue, not just delivering rehearsed answers. It's about listening actively, responding thoughtfully, and ensuring that your message resonates.

Instead of focusing on saying as much as possible, shift your attention to creating a real connection. This means being present in the moment, responding authentically, and matching the energy and tone of the conversation. The best podcast interviews feel like a natural exchange, where both the host and guest contribute to a compelling discussion that draws the audience in.

A strong connection with the host enhances the flow of conversation, making it more enjoyable and insightful. Likewise, connecting with the audience means understanding their interests and providing value—whether through personal stories, actionable insights, or fresh perspectives.

The most memorable guests are those who leave an impact, not by speaking the most, but by saying something that truly matters.

8. THE ROLE OF AUTHENTIC ENERGY

Authenticity is the magic ingredient that turns an ordinary interview into an unforgettable experience. When a guest is genuine, passionate, and present, it resonates with both the host and the audience.

Many guests think they need to have the "perfect" answers. But in reality, imperfections make you more relatable. If you:

- Stumble over a word? Laugh it off and keep going.
- Need a moment to think? Take a breath—silence adds weight to your words.
- Don't know an answer? Be honest. Say, "That's a great question—I've never thought about it that way before."

The audience connects with real people, not rehearsed robots.

Your energy sets the tone for the episode. If you bring enthusiasm, warmth, and openness, it lifts the conversation. Some ways to boost your presence:

- Smile while talking—yes, even in an audio-only podcast. Your voice naturally sounds more engaging.
- Use storytelling—facts tell, but stories sell.
- Be present—turn off distractions and immerse yourself in the conversation.

Your authenticity shouldn't stop at the interview. Make sure your online presence reflects who you were on the podcast. If you spoke about being passionate about leadership, does that show up in your LinkedIn posts? If you emphasized community, are you engaging with your audience on social media?

Authenticity isn't just a podcast strategy—it's a brand strategy that influences how people perceive and connect with you. In a world full of polished pitches and rehearsed messages, being real stands out. When you consistently show up as your true self, you build genuine trust with both the host and the audience. Listeners can sense when someone is being authentic versus when they're just saying what they think people want to hear.

By embracing authenticity, you create a memorable presence that extends far beyond a single episode. People don't just remember what you said—they remember how you made them feel. When you share personal stories, honest insights, and speak from a place of genuine passion, you establish a deeper connection. This connection translates into long-term relationships, whether with potential clients, collaborators, or even future podcast invitations.

Authenticity also reinforces brand consistency. If people hear you on multiple platforms and your message remains true to who you are, they develop confidence in you and your work. That trust is what leads to opportunities, business growth, and lasting impact. Being authentic isn't just about sounding good on a podcast—it's about showing up in a way that aligns with your values and leaves a lasting impression.

9. LEVERAGING YOUR PODCAST APPEARANCES

Leveraging your podcast appearances for growth is about more than just showing up and delivering a great conversation. A single interview has the potential to elevate your personal brand, expand your reach, and generate new opportunities, but only if you take intentional steps to maximize its impact. Too many guests treat a podcast interview as a one-time event, when in reality, it can be a long-term asset for your business and brand. By repurposing your content, engaging with the audience, tracking results, and building relationships, you can turn a single appearance into multiple touchpoints that keep working for you long after the episode airs.

One of the biggest mistakes guests make is not leveraging their interview content beyond the initial release. Instead of just sharing the episode once, repurpose it across different platforms to extend its lifespan. If the episode was recorded on video, create short clips or audiograms to share on social media. Highlight key takeaways in LinkedIn posts, Instagram carousels, Facebook reels or Twitter (X) threads. Write a blog post summarizing the episode's main points, expanding on the topics discussed, and linking back to the full episode. Send an email to your list with highlights from the conversation and a link to listen. Add the episode to your website, either in a dedicated "Media" section or as part of a blog post. If you regularly appear on podcasts, consider creating a "Featured On" section where visitors can see all your interviews in one place. Small actions like adding the podcast link to your email signature can also increase exposure. The goal is to transform one podcast episode into multiple pieces of content that reach different segments of your audience in different ways.

Engaging with the audience is just as important as sharing the episode. Podcast listeners often look for more ways to connect with guests they find interesting, so be proactive. Monitor and respond to comments on the host's social media posts about your episode. If listeners reach out with feedback, reply and start a conversation. Post about the episode on your own channels and encourage discussion by asking your audience what they found most valuable. Consider hosting a live Q&A on Instagram, LinkedIn, or Facebook to expand on the topics discussed in the episode and invite engagement. Join relevant Facebook or LinkedIn groups where the podcast's audience hangs out and participate in discussions related to your area of expertise. Engagement keeps you top of mind and builds trust with potential clients, partners, or followers.

Tracking and measuring the impact of your podcast appearances helps you refine your strategy and focus on opportunities that bring real results. Pay attention to website traffic to see if there are spikes after an episode airs. If you're promoting a service or product, use a unique promo code or dedicated landing page for each podcast to track conversions. Ask new clients, followers, or email subscribers where they first heard about you. If certain interviews drive more engagement, look for similar shows to appear on. If an episode performs well, consider doing a follow-up interview or deeper dive into the topic. Analyzing these metrics helps you understand which podcast appearances give you the best return on investment and how to optimize future opportunities.

One of the biggest benefits of podcast guesting is the potential for ongoing opportunities beyond the interview itself. If you build strong relationships with hosts, your appearance can lead to introductions to other podcast hosts, speaking engagements, partnerships, and more. After the episode airs, follow up with the host to express appreciation and keep the relationship warm. Offer to introduce them to other potential guests or invite them to be a guest on your platform if you have a podcast, blog, or event. Stay engaged with their content and continue the conversation beyond the episode. Many of the best networking opportunities happen because guests take the time to nurture connections rather than just moving on to the next show.

A well-planned podcast strategy can also help you monetize your appearances. If your goal is business growth, make sure each interview leads to tangible results. Provide a free resource or lead magnet to capture email subscribers. Offer an exclusive discount code for listeners who want to work with you. Mention a product, course, or service in a way that feels natural rather than sales-driven. Use storytelling to showcase the transformation your service provides rather than just listing its features. Follow up with engaged listeners who reach out after hearing you. Monetizing your podcast appearances is less about selling and more about demonstrating value in a way that makes people want to learn more.

The best podcast guests don't just record an interview and disappear. They maximize every appearance by repurposing content, engaging with listeners, tracking results, and building long-term relationships. With a little effort, one podcast appearance can turn into months of impact, growing your brand, expanding your audience, and creating ongoing business opportunities. Your voice has power—make every podcast appearance work for you.

10. START INVITING, START INTERVIEWING TODAY

Resources to start with (free versions)*

Spotify for Creators: free hosting and distribution
https://creators.spotify.com/

MEETN: 50mins free videoconference per meeting
http://www.meetn.com/

Calendly: schedule your guests
www.calendly.com

Resources for the advanced podcaster (paid options)*

PodMatch: find the perfect guest
https://bit.ly/podmatchinspires

PodcastAI.com
https://podcastai.com/

ModernIQs: get blog articles from transcripts in an instant
https://moderniqs.com/create-an-account/?res_aff=inspiredchoicetoday

---

* Some links may be affiliate links, which help support the growth and improvement of THE INSPIRED CHOICE TODAY

Wisdom Shared: Guiding Words from Guests

"You can be greater. Just enjoy the ride."- Norman Gräter

"A brand is not just the logo; it's an extension of you and how you show up."- Audrey Wiggins

"Don't let your education interfere with your education."
- John Taylor McEntire

"Your focus determines your reality."- Author Aaron Ryan

"Audiences resonate with authenticity. Content must be honest and transparent."- Venchele Saint-Dic

"I think just generally if you're a good person, you can inspire people."- Gillian Sneddon

"Peace and appreciation mean that we all have the same worth."- Annette Dernick

"The smallest change today on a daily basis is compounding to a big result in the end."- Monique Schmitz

"Make sure you leave time for yourself. Reclaim your time by automating and streamlining."- Kimberly Laverdure

"Sexuality and spirituality are one and the same."
- Lorna Gale

"I'm inspired to create all of these little circles around the world that eventually inspire the whole globe to go to a higher vibration."- Angela Sidlo

"We need to treat everyone for the value that they bring, and everyone brings a value."- John Verrico

"Forgiveness allows you to be the person you were always meant to be."- Katharine Giovanni

"The worst thing that ever happened to you often turns out to be a great gift."- Dr. Denise Brown

"I want to be a true me, the true version of me, as vulnerable and authentic as I possibly can."- Marie Öholm

"The more that you can ask for help from people around you and accept it from those that are offering help, the better off that you're gonna be."- Brian Elam

"Don't be afraid to seek other opinions and figure it out."- Dr. Edward Feinberg

"You have to give to receive. We have to be to become, and you have to aspire and get the best out of people."- Liliana Cavaliere

11. A HEARTFELT THANK YOU

This chapter is dedicated to expressing my deepest gratitude to everyone who has been part of this journey—the guests, listeners, and supporters who have made The Inspired Choice more than just a podcast, but a powerful movement. Over the course of 365 days, I recorded over 700 interviews, each one a testament to the incredible stories, insights, and wisdom shared by extraordinary individuals.

To my guests—thank you for showing up, sharing your truth, and inspiring countless others with your expertise and experiences. Every conversation has been a gift, and together, we've created something truly meaningful. To all the guests who have signed up for The Inspired Choice Chronicles: Horizons Ahead book experience—your commitment to leaving a legacy is deeply appreciated. You are part of something bigger, a ripple effect that will continue to inspire for years to come.

To my listeners—your support has fueled my persistence and passion. Knowing that these episodes have encouraged you to start your own journeys is the greatest reward. Thank you for showing up, listening, and sharing how this podcast has impacted you.

This journey is far from over. There will be more episodes, more stories, and more lives changed. And for those still waiting to start their own podcasting journey—the world is waiting for your voice.

Thank you for being part of this incredible experience. I'll see you in the next chapter—and in the next book.

With gratitude,
Caroline

12. ABOUT CAROLINE

Caroline Biesalski is a trailblazing *entrepreneur* and the host of the globally recognized podcast *The Inspired Choice*, ranked among the top **3% of podcasts worldwide** on Listen Notes. Her journey is a testament to the transformative power of courage, persistence, and intuition. Once labeled shy and introverted, Caroline overcame social phobia and self-doubt to create a platform that inspires people worldwide to step into their fullest potential.

Caroline's passion for empowering others stems from her own life experiences. After years of navigating a career in accounting and business, she rediscovered her childhood dream of hosting a show. This dream, rooted in her love for storytelling and connection, ultimately became a reality when she launched *The Inspired Choice*. Through her podcast, Caroline has interviewed hundreds of guests, sharing their wisdom and insights to inspire listeners to make bold, purposeful choices in their own lives.

As an *Inspired Choice Mentor*, Caroline helps individuals and teams transform self-limiting beliefs, align with their authentic selves, and take actionable steps toward achieving their dreams. She combines practical strategies with intuitive guidance, creating a unique approach that resonates deeply with her clients and audience alike.

Caroline's work is deeply influenced by principles from Bob Proctor's *Thinking into Results*, Napoleon Hill's *Laws of Success*, and her own lived experiences. Her ability to connect with people from all walks of life, paired with her authentic and relatable storytelling, has made her a sought-after coach, mentor, and host.

Today, Caroline continues to inspire and uplift through her podcast, mentoring, and writing. Her mission is simple yet profound: to help others recognize the power of their choices, embrace their uniqueness, and create lives filled with meaning and purpose.

Caroline lives by the mantra that every great journey begins with one inspired choice—and she invites you to start yours today.

The best is yet to come

- START NOW –

IT'S YOUR CHOICE

Authentic Stories, Surprising Lessons, and Practical Takeaways for Podcast or Business Starters empowering you to make impactful choices for both your personal and professional life.

Listen to The Inspired Choice podcast

www.podcast.inspiredchoice.today

Choose your platform: Apple Podcasts, Spotify, YouTube

Use the AI Chat to get answers about guests and topics

Become an inspiring interview guest by applying here

https://www.podmatch.com/hostdetailpreview/inspiredchoice

or send an E-Mail to interview@inspiredchoice.today

for any requests, feedback or further information about THE INSPIRED CHOICE Mentoring with Caroline Biesalski

See you in the next adventurous chapter of your life!

Yours,
Caroline Biesalski
Inspired Choice Mentor & Podcast Host